D0065000

False Gods,
Real Men

By the Same Author:

FALSE GODS, REAL MEN

NEW POEMS BY

Daniel Berrigan

The Macmillan Company

Collier-Macmillan Ltd., London

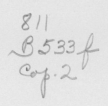

ACKNOWLEDGMENTS

"I am Never Complete," "The Unfinished Man," "Of Fair Love the Mother," "Somehow," "This Crucifix," and "The Wedding" first appeared in *Poetry*.

The poem "Somewhere the Equation Breaks Down" appeared originally in *The New Yorker*.

Other poems originally appeared in *Epoch, Continuum, Motive, Thought*.

To the Catonsville Nine

CONTENTS

False Gods,
Real Men

I

"I had a sense, only just under the skin, that I was at the end of something. I had been to Hanoi and seen the charnel house our military had made of a quite beautiful society. Easter Sunday, I visited a boy in Syracuse who had immolated himself in front of the Cathedral. He later died. And then there was Martin Luther King's murder. Suddenly I saw that my sweet skin was hiding out behind others."   *—Newsweek*

False Gods, Real Men

1.

Our family moved in 25 years from Acceptable Ethnic
through Ideal American
        (4 sons at war Africa Italy the Bulge Germany)
and Ideal Catholic
        (2 sons priests uncle priest aunt nun cousins
                              great-uncle etc. etc.)
But now; 2 priests in and out of jail, spasms, evictions,
                                    confrontations

      We haven't made a nickel on the newest war
      probably never again
              will think, proper
    with pride; a soldier! a priest! we've made it now!

What it all means is—what remains.
      My brother and I stand like the fences
          of abandoned farms, changed times
          too loosely webbed against
                  deicide   homicide
      A really powerful blow, a cataclysm
          would bring us down like scarecrows.
      Nature, knowing this, finding us mildly useful
          indulging also
          her backhanded love of freakishness
             allows us to stand.

      The implication
          both serious and comic;
            wit, courage
      a cry in the general loveless waste

          something
        than miracle
          both more and less

. . . did conspire to enter, disrupt, destroy
draft files of the American Government, on
the 17 day of May . . .
—Indictment

2.

Among the flag poles
wrapped like Jansenist
conventicles
with rags
at half mast
(alas for sexual
mortmain) the wooden poles
on high but
dry

3.

We did yes we did your Honor
impenitent—
while legitimate cits
newts   bats   foxes
made congress
in formerly
parks and green swards
rutting   earnestly drilling
tooth and claw
galling   inserting
industrious   inventive
nitroglycerin, nuclear
instrumentalities

4

4.

We fools and felons
went on a picnic
apples   quince   wines   hams   swimsuits
loaves   fishes   noonday relics and traces
badminton   watery footsoles   infants
thereafter impounded!

An FBI agent estimated at least 600 indi-
vidual files were in the two huge wire bas-
kets carried from Local Board No. 33 and
set fire in the parking lot.

—AP dispatch

5.

Then foul macadam
blossomed like rosemary
in the old tapestry
where unicorns deigned
to weave a fantasy
truer I swear than

6.

Judge Mace his black
shroud   his skeletal
body & soul
whose veins decant
vapors to turn the
innocent eye
dry as the dead.

7.

Indicted
charged with creating
children   confusion
legerdemain   flowers
felonious picnics.
Jews in Babylon
we sit and mourn
somewhere in Mace's
mad eyes' spaces

> When a United States judge sentenced two
> of the pacifists to six years in Federal prison
> . . . he clearly ignored sound discretion. The
> powers of the bench include the power to
> fix sentences on those found guilty, but
> they do not include the right to impose
> punishment out of all proportion to the
> crime.
>   —*The New York Times*

8.

The cure for foul dreams
is day, dawn. For chimera's claw marks
flesh! For false gods, real men
for Honor Mace, his insect secret, tears
that freshen, springs. For foul, fair
say it, shout it; fair for unfair, in courts of law-
    lessness. For pulpits
                (rotten as
    wormwood, the propped skeleton
his thimble fingers grasping like throats

6

book and eagle, flag and altar stone)
                    O you
dishonored priest, your retinue
    the last, least men of this
        most sorrowful world!

> "I have tried all the conventional and legal
> forms of protest to little or no avail," says
> Philip, who argues that both Christ and Paul
> allowed the possibility of civil disobedience
> when man's law counters God's.
> —*Time*

9.

TO PHILIP

Compassionate, casual as a good face
(a good heart goes without saying)
someone seen in the street; or
infinitely rare, once, twice in a lifetime

that conjunction we call brother or friend.
Biology, mythology cast up clues.
We grew together, stars made men
by cold design; instructed

sternly (no variance, not by a hair's
breadth) in course and recourse. In the heavens
in our mother's body, by moon and month were whole
men made. We obeyed then, and were born.

II

The following verses were written on the
spot, in the course of a trip to Hanoi,
January 31–February 18, 1968.
The reader may be sure that
references to actual persons, living or dead,
are purely intentional—indeed willful.

Waiting: Vientiane

The birds of dawn are crying, drawing
        the great sun into conflict
    a contested light

the bloody challenge taken, the spurred leap, roof after roof.

        Visualize such a bird
     as you imagine the sun
           a black carapace
      a fruit bitter as limes
            a bull studded with flags
a guerrilla striking while the iron is hot.

        SUN
     who alone cocks eye (eyeing that cock)
           and not
     burns his socket blind; from his
intolerable equinox, seeing in the sea
         himself rampant, eye to eye
    lives in that cry nor turns to stone
            nor no, shall die

Prayer

I left Cornell
with half a wit; six mismated socks
ski underwear, a toothbrush,
passport, one hundred good
green dollars, their faces
virtuous as ancestors,
the chamois sack
Karl Meyer gave me years ago, handmade
by dispossessed Georgia Negroes.

Later, dismay; no Testament.
I must construct, out of oddments, abrasions,
vapor trails, dust, pedicabs
three crosshatch continents, Brooks Brothers embassies
their male models dressed to kill—

all He meant and means. I touch
shrapnel and flesh, and risk my reason
for the truth's sake, an ignorant hung head.

Man of one book, stand me in stead.

Night Flight to Hanoi

In a bar in Vientiane
they said to us
like Job's mockers;
thanks to your own ever loving bombers
you may never see
the northern lights, Hanoi.

Then, by bat radar
we crawled that corridor
blind as bats,
a wing and a prayer.

Came in!
the big glare of a klieg eye
held us, hooked, death's open season.
We held breath, fish
baited, not landed.

Ended; the pale faces of flowers
said suddenly, out of season
something than death other, unuttered.

Exiles we went in
safe kept, cherished by strangers.

Alert

The sirens are loosed on Hanoi
a Stalingrad
ringed round, rained upon, fired—

the air force calls
like a whistle of game cocks at dawn
like a song of songs
like the embassy eagle
on whom the sun never sets
the celibate, the almost
       (for self will
       for lack of an equal
       killer or climber)

extinct of its kind.

Bombardment

Like those who go aground
willfully, knowing that man's
absurd estate can but be bettered
in the battering hands of the gods—

yet mourning traitorously the sun and moon
and one other face, and heat of hearth—

went under
like a blown match. The gases flare on the world's combustible
flesh.

Children in the Shelter

Imagine; three of them.

As though survival
were a rat's word,
and a rat's end
waited there at the end

and I must have
in the century's boneyard
heft of flesh and bone in my arms

I picked up the littlest
a boy, his face
breaded with rice (his sister calmly feeding him
as we climbed down)

In my arms fathered
in a moment's grace, the messiah
of all my tears. I bore, reborn

a Hiroshima child from hell.

Flowers

A flower is single jeopardy—
only one death; matrons' scissors, dogs,
natural deflowering; choose. Meantime
dare time and wind and war. Be

no one's metronome, discount
in a lover's hand, the ways
we die—routine, wrong analogy.

I start these words because
a girl on a bicycle
swaying

bears a few flowers
homeward through war, a double jeopardy.
I held
breath for her, her flowers, on the wheel of fire,
the world, no other.

Sentries, we passed, no countersign

except *good-bye*
forced   first   last word of all.

Song

The maids sing at their scrubbing
the cooks at the stove—
shame women; such lightness of mind
ill becomes; think rather on
Death   Judgment   Heaven   Hell

the names of the bombers
that bear in their skull
your names, memorized in fire.

Progress in Rural Development:
A Lecture on Privies, and a Gift
to Our Countrymen

In the municipal hospital, in the bone-chilling cold
the dispassionate voices, Viet and English, unfolded
an invincible case for improvement of village privies.

Doubters, we sniffed with our senses the odorless faeces
achieved by new methods of drying. We stood.
The photographer readied. Passed to the doctor's hands

and to ours, and on through ten thousand miles
into marveling America (and carefully constructed
as a boat in a bottle, as a model of Model T)
      that gift, that two-seated wonder.

My Name

If I were Pablo Neruda
or William Blake
I could bear, and be eloquent

an American name in the world
where men perish
in our two murderous hands

Alas Berrigan
you must open those hands
and see, stigmatized in their palms
the broken faces
you yearn toward

you cannot offer
being powerless as a woman
under the rain of fire—
life, the cover of your body.

Only the innocent die.
Take up, take up
the bloody map of the century.
The long trek homeward begins
into the land of unknowing.

The Pilots, Released

1.

When I think of you it is always (forgive me)
of disposable art; 50 designs drawn from the damp woodcut
of 50 States, the physiognomy of camp—

Innocence (mom), *pietàs* (pop), the household gods
guarding the gates guarded by you, O proxies
for all providence   Saigon to

Rio to Congo   your chilling logic
draws blood   a blood bank   a blank bloody
check drawn on the living
                              who thereupon
          here   there   and tomorrow by all accounts
                    are dead

2.

The trouble with innocence
is itself, itself in the world—
the GI who had a wife
but never imagined one
had children true to form
whose lives described
like dance or geometry
the outer edge, drawn there
in diametric blood—
thus far love, and no further.

3.

In the old moth-eaten plane   (one-eyed—heroic
as a pirate carp)   the youngest pilot
lived it over and over   roped like an animal
to the water wheel   drawing up
buckets   water   blood   honey   spleen
lug and tug   104 days in solitary
loneliness   near madness   interrogations
brainwashing of that brain already
hung   high and dry as a woodcut

of himself   by himself; *Our Boy; Spit, Polish, Literal Death.*

III

Time, gentlemen!
    a diary of sorts, an idea—
  eyes require faces
         ears voices
      (I hear you)
      wrists hands
              hands no weapons
  poems you

Salvation History

I had a nightmare—
the rickety shack brought down
I was sheltering in;
from sleep to death
gone, all coped in dream

What then? I had never lived?
it well might be.
Without friends, what is man?
their noon and moon, my own

Without friends—what?
dead, unborn, my light
quenched, never struck.

The piteous alternatives
life simulates!
streets haunt, faces hang

but I mark
like an unquenched man
merciful interventions

a clean end or beginning
someone to die for   some love to sing

Obit

We die perplexed, dwarfed by the petty
crises we thought contained, controlled

showing like frayed pockets, space within
without, for loss.
                          Pain in eyes, a ragged
animal before the gun;
                                    muzzily—
can death do any harm
life hasn't done? maybe
                                    dreamily   death
turns old dogs
into fish   hillsides   butterflies
                          teaches a new
trick or two

There Must Be a God

I thought I heard
my own life say it
and the crumbling streets
and alkys mumbling, and the shot landscape
of my youth; gone—
trees, sweetness, euphoria

Yet in someone's hair or hand
a rose, blown and ragged,
a victory somewhere
like a torch in the hands of a runner
beat, dying, but on his feet.

Let there be a God
is man's big news;
let Him show as much heart
as a good man musters;
leave us alone
to make do, fumble about, fret through;
He must leave us our sins
to learn and ravel;
sweat, start false, feint, dissimulate.

Let Him be a dying vine, a back door
marked "colored only"
day old bread, wino's wine.
Let Him "stand with the fate
of the majority of men."
A shepherd, if He like folklore,
like the Roman gypsies
at Christmas time
blowing their big sheep bladders
like an ass's brag
crying, not Christmas
but their own sores and rags.

O incarnation is a hard word.
There is some flesh I could not take.
On my way to a Bowery wedding
the Bowery sty;
in a Bellevue ward
sour lees, sour wine;
uptown east, spiffy aseptic dogs
parading cloud nine;
the doormen's preternatural fishy stare—

ah wilderness! He marvels
I am more astonished
with what I find here
than with what I bring!

The Clock in the Square

Ineffectuals
chained, reined to time's beaten track—
simulacra all, strangers to action, passion

strike the hour, lurch away
pale as linen
the pharaohs of long refusal.

Some Sort of Explanation,
Better Than None

I cultivate a grin
that takes into account
a rear end
bruised
by an ass's iron shoe

Meantime
that knock you hear
is death's drumstick
tapping his forehead 3 times
with the knowing look
of woody woodpecker;

for this, and other
prudential courtesies
    of wind & weather
    of lack and luck
    of the fair fall
    of bones them bones—

love life!

A Further Question

The world
appalls, astounds, evades.
A flower is drama

dawn a god.
a dead hand presses me
fighting for my last breath
to fill with stolen
time, his vial.

The book warms like a mind
under living hands,
runs like a pip to blade,
rains like a Sinai cloud.

Am I then no more
than a philosopher's naked stone—
reductive shape
of the fabulous world?

a mocking Pharisee
before his titular idol
his stone ego, fabricated
god and man?

No. A phoenecian woman
borne under in issue of blood
touches
in hot faith, living flesh

cries piteously (and is heard)
O heal!

Somehow

I kiss a book sometimes
like a bride or the gospel
or land, after wild seas
grant me a man again.

The things we love!
women, the truth, planets—

like flowers through ruins
like brides through deserts
like shore through murderous mist—

out of wreckage and rancor. Somehow!

Come Alive

I had lost everything for a year
a stick in a blind hand—
conundrums, fantasy

the blind hand struck, the stick
stuck rotting in rich ground.
Four seasons come and gone.

Imagine a face? summon
sustenance, vision, up from that ground?

My mind took no fire
from fiery truth; my hands hung
like hanged necks, dead, dead as a show.

But the children of Birmingham
clairvoyant, compassionate among the dead—

I see you all night long.
Dawn winds freshen. The cock
makes children by the clock.
The trees lift up their dawn.

Somewhere the Equation Breaks Down

between the perfect
(invisible, Plato said)
and the imperfect
that comes at you on the street,
stench and cloth and fried eyes;
between the wired bones of the dead
stuttering, shamed
and the marvelous lucid spirit
that moves in the body's spaces
a rainbow fish behind glass—
decide. O coincide!

November 20, 1965

Subway faces beheaded
in the blade of your eyes.
Life? step in and be
lost.
All heaven's bells
nod in accord
like Botticelli curls;
yes O yes

I think of my father and mother;
their dignity measures
the horror—
that leap
marked like a third rail's
mortal sputter;
danger!

They leapt, and live;
the stranger's wounds succored
the lost child safe in arms.

I Wonder, Do You

                know
        the things you make seem
                possible?
        My flesh ends; be-
            neath, a toehold on hell;
        ahead, a divining rod; above
                a hairy
        pumpkin with a grin
                knifed in.
        Life; my cry, your gift
                —else
            head to feet, I
        rot like fish in voracious air;
            the rod that greened and perked
        on rumor of fresh springs
                die
        like an issueless king's
            dry stick, wet dream

Peacemaking Is Hard

(FOR JIM AND SALLY DOUGLASS)

hard almost as war.
The difference being one
we can stake life upon
and limb and thought and love.

I stake this poem out
dead man to a dead stick
to tempt an Easter chance—
if faith may be
truth, our evil chance
penultimate at last

not last. We are not lost.

When these lines gathered
of no resource at all
serenity and strength,
it dawned on me—

a man stood on his nails

as ash like dew, a sweat
smelling of death and life.
Our evil Friday fled,
the blind face gently turned
another way, toward life

a man walks in his shroud

IV

Recent events
       of practically no import
but which a single eye
       might barter itself blind
just to see

The Trip

It was a foolish ricochet
of ignorance off good intention.
I came on the New Haven railroad
to visit a friend in Darien Hospital.
The New Haven
is like the emergency room
of a public hospital, toward the close
of a catastrophic day.

Or so it seemed that day.
Innocent, feckless, men
hawked their wares
with overkill drunken skill;
all, all aboard; no haven.

The New Haven; four sailors
(I am accident prone)
staked their claim near me.
One of them strummed a guitar,
a passable voice.
They worked through ten or twelve
gentle songs.
Then things turned around, turned ugly;
the songs, the air
sour as a drunk's distemper.

I hope
I am not grown hopeless
seeing things often go
from ripe to rot.
That ripeness they say is all—
how rare!

sometimes, toward dawn, it comes—
a hand like my father's hand

brown, veinous, streaked
pops
the first prize Farmer's Pride
into my mouth.
I eat
as much as a man eats
whose life, a free load,
bodes ill, brings in
no harvest cash.

Seminar

One speaker
an impeccable
Californian
impelled to explain

The Chinese Belong In China
The Russians In Russia.
we however—
messiah, oversoul
a pink   muscled   clear-eyed
Texan dream
fumigating
Hanoi privies
from above—
napalm   jigger bombs   gas
God's saniflush, in sum—

The gentleman was
four square as State
or the pentateuch;
sans beard, rope sandals, foul talk, pot—
a fire extinguisher
on Pentecost day;
exuding good will
like a mortician's convention
in a plague year.

Indeed yes.
There is nothing sick
(the corpse said)
about death.
Come in.

A Hard Day in the City, Followed by Fun and Games

(FOR S. S.)

One would have thought
breeding, money, a swimming pool out back
and running free, five beautiful children

would compensate—but what?

the price our lives
like it or not, exact; other forms and smells

cast in the face, than roses.

O nights ago
when lightning broke
we ran like demons
three hundred yards to the columned shelter
the big house furred, lit like a st. bernard's eyes

across the sweet grass, ran
from sight, from sightlessness
            our desperate hearts' last dash

Independence Day and After

Our old Alma
battens down her hatches;
the Alumni Vets of Freedom
come for that big annual
Clan Wake—hurray!

the day when the flag
wears itself
as a peacock's brain a
gorgeous inviolate tail
no one (by God and us)
ever will have a piece of!

July 5; rake the scorched lawns
send up old glory again, a
shipwreck signal;
                    above
the color bars, the tricky
stars
          One evening light
breathes free
the heavens
weep and laugh together
psycho and sane
for human folly

An Old Wife Remembers

We started in a clapboard house that year
on a turnpike next to a Cutty Sark sign.
The bottle stood up, big as a bum's dream.

He'd say; just wait, tonight after ten you'll see.

Well yes. The bottle lit up, started,
tipped, poured light like a firebrand
I thought, the Empire State Building
tumbling on you, millions of goodies,
the water coolers, the heating plant, look out!

O the visual aids we had that year!

The light crossed his brows
red then green, a go ahead. We went under, gently, fiery.

There was a story somewhere—
trolls lived under a waterfall, boys trod a furnace. You
O you were mine.

1967—Vietnam

Two hands (fixation, horror)
raised in the stone doorway
falter, let drop
wine and fire from the empty cup.

You avail—nothing.

Something? tell
the bread that failed, the circuses that fell.

Paris Revisited: The Ile Saint Louis

One willow, vast, a mast of that old brig,
another
spouting fronds like a river god.
I kissed them, where time like a rotten wine skin
broke and ran.
Walking the old cobbles, time's odor
like fresh rain, old wine;
I cried in exaltation
                    Born here!

A poem comes easily
walking home, soaked to the skin
behind two lovers
their hands cold and wet
joined under lamps;
between them, the speaking stream.

my heart crying like theirs;
                    born, born here!

Paris Revisited: At Mass

The monks streamed in
like banners or Dunsinane or the sea.
A pop Christ overhead
hulked big as a billboard.

Then
faith
or the street sounds
or my own absurd mind
set a metaphor going;
a scrubbed manure cart
loaded with spring flowers
weaving through a rutted town—
a procession ablaze with ten kinds of fire.

And the smell!
depending on the wind, depending
on a man's expectation—
raffish, stinging
a barnyard cart of manure—
or a gentle mocking gift of Eve
a crown of morning glories
a transmutation
over a privy pit.

Faith, yes;
barnyard, Versailles garden.

Trip Through Michigan

The poem started,
Pure in a time of toads,
a jewel in a pismire—

No. I mean to come
if time is merciful, to a simpler word;

a vegetarian, *since I work among the poor*
and most men never taste meat!
Sleeping on the floor, glorying, brimming
like a Hebrew hero, a full vessel.
I thought of Blake's god,
touching the universe at all points,
a child within a hoop, all light and exaltation;
a vine, groaning with life, a eucharist tree—
not a sour drop, no sour ground
underfoot.

We drove the Michigan roads
like Jonahs in God's belly.
The moon came on like a prophet's lamp.
Behind, the neanderthals, their posters
"Judas" in red, three goons bearing a cross,
our meeting broken up like a puppet nightmare;
back to Wayne
marveling, bewildered, beat.

Life in the whale
big as an island cave!
We
pumping him on like a heart
pushing his lungs like a bellows

bound for a port
sealed like ambergris in some secret brain.

Turning the Picture Book

(A EUCHARISTIC PROCESSION)

Your unreal presence in a photo, passed
down a Spanish street;
a long line of surpliced priests
receding.
One half the page was this;
an honor guard
bayonets massed, a street barricade.

Believe me, gorgeous bird
we were not hungry for your heart.
There you went
a millionaire's heir,
Prague's golden boy,
the Czar's easter egg,
a baby resembling bread.
And hell's angels,
your blank-eyed muscle men
keeping you safe
from a kidnapping.

O if I were you
I would strike them down
like Pilate's bullies
and stand and break
myself in two
like Samson's heart
in his own hands. Myself,
like bread
like a hero's heart.

A Civil Rights Demonstration

That morning I weighed
like a Dickens brat
no expectations. Would I march
capped in bells like Christ's fool, or Christ?

who walked with us
borne on what wind?
driven Jews, sere in vein and eye?
Sharpeville's seventy, brave in red ribbons?

O who will turn
dust to a man on march? I taste in mouth
the dust of Jews, the *durst not kill* of prophets
a taste that kills.

Bread loaf king
shelved, mouldering; a churchmice clergy start

cut, flee for cover. See how they run
like field mice under the teeth or scythe. Like men.

On the Turnpike

Who loaded history's pig iron
pack, bade a man shoulder it
and die of it and
     if he could
rise in the shoddy world?

Thus; a monger man, his sack
big as a shroud or sail, trailing
the stinking phosphorous waste.

I saw or half saw from the sky way stream
Hiroshima, Easter garden, a rag man
poking the filth for bread
     and heard
one lost word on that witch's wind
riding the vacuum, its own

good news or foul, who knows, a rose?

Bergamo: Instructions for Going Forth

(News item.
In a fresh dug crypt
under the new seminary,
they are constructing
a 2,000-seat church
against the day
when John XXIII of Bergamo
is declared saint.)

1.

Alas if a man's death
toss his bones
like unlucky dice
among medicine men
hawkers spivs

might he not
cast a more thoughtful eye
on other
exits, intercessions?

    birds of paradise
    long distance runners
    acrobats   wandering clerks

    invitations   dawns
    catherine wheels   the sun's
    love poetry   death by fire

    a land (at last) of no
    morticians?
    sandalwood pyres   ashes

borne upon streams
from the heartland

2.
Little remaining
of the old peasant pope;
iconoclast hands
turning his dust vilely to gold.

Yet on the old road upward to the old city
cobbles steam in the sun after a dawn rain
like smoking loaves—

a passionate life, a horn of harvest
bread, bread, sustenance for all!

Guess What I Almost Lost Today

A sidelong hairy look
a mouth like a silk purse—

he held it tight
in six-fingered hands

weighing the king's eyeballs,
honest though God be thief.

I got it back and breathed it in
safe and scarce.

It screwed its face to a fist
like a babe at the nipple

what did I mean in hell or heaven
bartering the unborn away

that way   without a vote?

The Wedding

(FOR DAVID AND CATHERINE MILLER)

Make way, make way! the poor
sit for the wedding feast; syrup onions beans
a chunk of bread.
                        The guitars
strum it like throats; come to the marriage day!

And I thought; you must take it whole,
you must swallow it, acrid, disastrous,
the sour air, the clangor, the revolting
loveless, heartless, unjust mass,
weights pressing the heart into weird misshape,
the imponderable brutal load that makes
brutes of us all; neutral minds,
stocks and stones; rapacious ominous law
nine points of dispossession, faces
beaten under night sticks;
                        the churches
gripping like locust shells the tegument of life—

Don't speak of love until everything is
lost; antagonism, agony!
no vow, no faith, the wedding bread
spoiled, scattered like chaff; the bride
a whoring recusant.
                        O who will make
amends, my love?
                        I climbed up
step after iron step, inferno
into your eyes. I have married
sight of your face, that took
all this and me beside
                        for groom, for the bride's
evil and good, sickness and hope and health.
Yes.

I have learned from you
                              YES
                                   when
                                        no
unmans me like a knife, turns
like an evil lock, the incarnate bridal door.

Diary

(EASTER, 1966)

I hadn't walked the tow path in Central Park
for six months, having flapped southward
like a lame duck, under circumstances
that yield here to self-censoring.

I went; the Park gave scarcely a shrug,
the big body
autumnal, luxuriant,
a vague disinterest in eye
a hung up blear of smog
a rare fitful candor, a dog's
intelligence, an old horse's look. O sun!

Absent, the Park was in my heart
not noble, remorseful, remembering;
a wink, a New York shrug.
Nevertheless, went with me
an animal shadow, all its animals—
seals, weeping
the absurdest tears of all creation—

I called good night
that last time, November 20. The sea lion
a shmoo's dream of beatitude, a feast afloat
turned on me
his rheumy uncle's eye;
time for all that
time to envy eagles, clouds like slow birds,
gulls slow as paper from the huffing stacks
time for return. He'd see me.

Southward, I thought of paeons to the Park.
Rio children had a park in mind
mud pies, dust cake, the hominoids like children.
Alas, their bones scrawled in the dust

alas, and the winds took the word away, as years
our bones

Home again, I visit the seal;
his majesty, cold in his ingrown mask
tight in his poorhouse trousers,
promulgates
the good life, laissez-faire,
49 brands of fish.

Ponderous
half in, half out of the water
his leather flipper
tapping the sea wall like God the Father
or Teddy Roosevelt
WELCOMES ME, NAME OF ALL!

O the Park descends on the city
like a celestial napkin, as if heaven
were all of earth, the fusty smell
of animals in arks, of cornered lives and deaths.
What is our freedom, Peter?
Obedience.
You have answered well;

I give you—exodus.
Wandering Jew
you have a Jew for God.
The Park
unreal as real estate
under the flood
bears you away, ashore:
The city!

V

People, people
the muted quarrels with existence
that go on
in corners and high wires and round places
where hearts will not play the angles
the daring die
and circles go round in alleluia

I Must Pour Life

Bronze celibates
thread space like spiders. Hands
inoffensive as lizard's
wave effete farewell
to arms, to full-blooded
speech, to country matters.

I saw a priest once
mired in his people's lives
hunching a hundred-pound sack
up four flights of stairs
pulling for breath on the top landing.

What then is health?
I must pour
hell's black humors in the dawn cup
transubstantiate their vileness in that blood
hate cannot sour, envy
thin to a whey.

say *I am sick*
implore *come heal me.*

John Anderson My Jo John

Men cannot pluck or wear
the mystery that bears no flower here;
or does, but we
no flowering eyes to see.

Yet take my flesh's word—
it roots in me, draws blood;
some death
or birth perhaps. I have no word.

A Saint on the Dash Board:

        to hear. But not too near.
I had a friend once, failed
for dogged solicitude,
playing shadow, crawling in my skin.

Leave kids their sins.
Let them cut their sails
badly, toward shoals.
Better wrong
than tolled, right and left.
The saint
toils on as he toiled
the chancy road where he
like we, find or not
the white pebble under a toad's rot.

Life is the very devil.
Who needs a plastic conning smile
to say so or no?

A Severe Critic, a Kind of Answer

Of course, violence!
the rose exists to be torn from its bush

color, form, defenselessness, all invite
        violation, celebration,
death, apotheosis, the breast of the beloved.

But it is one thing, you agree
        to pluck a flower
                as a large gracious way
        beyond, not tantamount to
words words words

And another, to assume
        the iron mercenary stance
                of Bully Boy
        his mount
                letting go like Pantagruel

        a defoliant hissing
                over the rose beds

while with steely savior's eye
        astride the brutal shoulders
                our boy
scans the horizon for a bigger game.

West Side Story

A Broadway hash joint, a Puerto Rican
short orders *2 burgers with cheese,*
2 without; onions, ketchup

in 4 minutes flat, with style, verve, and
a rare smile in a sour borough.

Far from Gracie Mansion and the gentle Sheep
Meadow. He hasn't smelled roses in years

but he wears them. While
nightmares hustle like rats
a night's undoing
                              he feeds modestly
(a few inferior loaves, a few
greasy fish) the city poor.

Winner? we have no other.
In a bad time, blessed
are you, for blessing me.

And What Is Man

Not like the rich
a fist of worms for a heart;
nor like the poor
consumed with making do,
rancor at dawn, futility at dusk

say; like a slum child
in a filthy yard—
a spool, a few crossed sticks

something different from himself—
the doll wound on a bobbin
almost talks back,
almost stalks away.

Was this the way He meant us?
meddlesome
proud, not docile

to stand to Him, thwart, amaze Him still!

I Am Never Complete

(FOR AL AND BARBARA UHRIE)

A man, a woman, their love
in the lower East Side
like Shakespeare added to
a sentient row of minds.
Make room, the books whisper.
The majestic mind, as they move
makes room for its counterparts.
I am never complete, history
awaiting its further emblem.
Among children, junkies, pushcarts
a lover's heart searches out my heart.

Facing It

Who could declare your death, standing
obedient as Stylites, empty as death's head
moving gently as the world's
majestic sun into night?

It was a hollow death; men
dread it like a plague. Thieves die this way,
charlatans, rejects. A good man's thought recoils;
his best years, aspiration, children

beckon a different road. To grow old yes,
gently one day to stop breathing, home and faces
drifting out of mind. Abrupt violence even
he can countenance, a quick mercy on disease

but not this, not this. The mother's face
knotted, mottled with horror.
A vision,
a few men destroyed.

It is always like this; time's cruel harrowing,
furies at the reins of fortune
wild horses dragging
the heroic dishonored body on time's ground.

O for an act of God! we cry, before death utterly
reduce to dust
            that countenance, that grace and beauty.

But
come wild hope, to dead end. War, murder,
anguish, fratricide.

No recourse. The case of Jesus Christ
is closed. Make what you will

70

desire, regret, he lies
stigmatized, a broken God
the world had sport of.

Risen? we have not turned that page.

To the Prisoners

(MEXICO CITY)

I saw the iron rings about the necks
of tortured prisoners
in frescoes by Rivera, in the National Palace.
Above, monkey-faced monks
held to the dying, the lying crucifix.

Behold, the iron on other necks now!
the cleric's collar, like a spiked mastiff
warns; *keep off*
color, music, sexual sweetness, spontaneity
passionate use of the world!
a black coverall
begins at wrists and ankles
like sacking on the dolls
that in my childhood, began to be true
at neck, hands and feet; all between
homunculus of straw, alas!

When they had locked the prisoners' irons
(the guide book says)
the executioners came forward
a line of purposeful apes
Platonic, implacable . . .

it is our history. In the mercado
you choose from a basket;
dolls' head, hands, feet
and in another booth
sacking and shredded straw
to fashion
that five-pointed rustling star
sew it to limbs
that walk, gesticulate—
a blank-eyed verisimilitude,
Tissot's still born first born.

Madame's son?
we will never know; the crotch
is decently stitched
sterile as an armpit.

Our testament forbids
(despite the bloody hands
that stain the text)
torture, murder, the bloody curriculum taken like rare meat.
I am so apart from the fresco,
at the same time
I lie within it!
A friend, a psychologist
half serious, called me
his "troubled adolescent."
I had not sought him out; he found me
lightheaded in Mexican air
weeping
for organized madness
a half starved dog
guarding the dead flesh of my brother.
Better, I thought, among men, a dog
than among dogs, a killer.

Every day, every day for three years
efficient as a madman's
three-year plan
for renewal of the earth
the bombers go out
renewing the earth.

You may say; the descent of the beast
if it be motivated, moral, compassionate,
ensures
the survival of all.

It is indeed to the advantage
of the king of beasts
to weave analogies
from the lives of beasts.
Bear with me. I am

neither sawdust doll nor brutish monk.
I wear
foolish collar, sacking
the circus pie
of a clown whose passionate will
persuades him to be useless,
whose death
sheriffs, cardinals, generals
conspire, in the old moralities
to bring to pass—
a providence, a use.

O church and state
my church, O mausoleum;
state
the stated clerk of death
I take in my two hands
the tortured mother, the blighted child
the prisoner's face
lax as a wax work—
Christ's tears have dulled
the sheriff's rage, sharpened
the doll's dead eyes.
Surprise!
(we have his word)
we burst like straw
our sexual death
we sow like autumn fools
hope in the leprous furrow.

Agamemnon

I sought to imperate joy
like a child
along a shore, in places above the sea;
seeding
primary mercies
rainfall, evening.

my brothers   my brothers
is any of you like me
a king home from crusade
his bath   his bath
a gauze of waters
laid over and under
new flesh on his crying bones

O deceived
somnolent
after long absence; hearing
the masked chorus

the king's house stands
firm as covenant
never O never shaken

then
the perfidious eyes
the net
hissing like nemesis

Help Me Someone

I should like to know please
the name of that girl
lauded in some obscure corner
of the press

dead in Paris
buried in Père Lachaise cemetery,
dedicated it was said, to the common
life of man

an American girl
solicitous for the sick
succoring outcasts
showing the city of light
an unaccustomed
incandescence.

Why then the question?
except that her bones
make
so small a sound
in the noiseless sockets
of history

except that the dead
press
upon us

and *learn! learn!* is the law
whereby we stand
and they
cut free

This Crucifix

        never a miracle!
its man
clings there, life's last straw
death's
crude analogate.

Cold man
we push the gospel
at a dead heart.

Where great love is
are miracles, the saints say
who are held
in principle, to no proof.

Days I turn
to cry the healer for some hint.
From dying eyes
there flies
a silver cock
to taste the bitter air

foul   foul.
and someday—*fair?*

Of Fair Love the Mother

Panic of dark minds sounds
about the level brows, the austere skull
that harbors like a shell
the inmost mystery of all years.
Sternness, compassion in those eyes;

come near, the quick and dead. Be born of me.

Saint Francis

Sometimes
I come through
like the first note
of a trumpet
fired with morning
round as a Saturn ring
hot and cold
as a virgin's dream—

highest C

off your radar your purported
ears
stuffed like mouths
with yesterday's omelettes
trussed like turkeys
groaning;
they have stolen
alas my
heart my
gizzard my
2 rare
unstrung pearls.

No; there went ME;
my heart's thrum thrum my
gizzard's auld lang syne my
pearls' sound of milk
warm from the tit, hitting
(squall) the cat's eyeball

unheard unheard as love
mostly on
Thanksgiving Christmas your
trussed capons your
burning babes.

No—
the sweet spontaneous
animals hear
me and
fear not and
draw
near.

Unfinished

he walks with his winter shadow.
He is all hoar's breath,
health; he strides, a visible
heart, the sun's hair spring.
Who calls him incomplete?

The artist does;
four crossed bones, a rusted cage,
hardware, kinetics. An argument
too easily won.
                    Then—
who calls him man?

I will wait his death
I will touch him to a Jew.

Junk man, skies fall on you
a rain of glory, a fire fall—
new ways into the world.

To the Jesuits

you have surpassed your myths
                        you are
all intellectual patience
                        you have seen
vanity and seasons
                        drown drown in their witches'
                        trial by water
your august temper
                        moves in the world
austere   uncozening
I know myself   only
                        in you.
Yes   I wed you   conscience   reason

But then
            will the bride give welcome?

            Père Rasles missioner
                        saw
            in English colony towns
                        staked out
            like burls or turnips
                        the heads
            of Indian squaws—
                        Puritan squeamishness
            the price of never
                        touching!
            the Jesuit, his gentle prose,
                        his hands
            laid upon flesh   like flowers

O you will never
give back to man his defamed
untouchable beauty
                        except you renounce

                  all   all
sour passion
Puritan will

                    to judge   to have done
                    the untidy   venereal
                    rampant   besotted
                    weed-ridden WORLD!
                         (that
                         alas or alleluia
                         enters most subtly
                         furrow and marrow
                                              a blue

                         pollen on green
                         roses   a black
                         flesh upon white—
Murderous times, a gentle man   Père Rasles
his health   his natural humor
                              (Then
those portentous brows
                         those stern messianic lips
NO LIQUOR NO CURSING NO JOY NO DANCING NO—
such a NO to life!   faces
like traps upon living limbs
                         closed upon NO)

Him they killed too
after much conniving   and near miraculous
rescue by his "savages"

Père Rasles! celebrate the mind's true grain
          health   humor   rightness   capacity!

                    Then
          O will you   take me
          whose health is sickness
          whose rich is poor
          whose better   worse?

                    the Puritan No!
                    that void excess   that
                    wintry will

                                              83

enclave of death   that god
fleecing the world   a flower
he could not bear or wear

No! unless
                    O say it—
        YES!

Somebody's Easter Goes Like This

(MARY SPEAKS)

Of course one wanted to play valiant—
the books advised, consented. Troy's bogus goddess,
the Eurasian sledding her son's body
pemican or cordwood, home. But the sun hangs
like a frozen star; it claps
hand to blind eye, Tiresias. Portents?
evasion of that will, hard as hell's roadbed
telling the way awry and right, crying *choose!*

descending that road homeward, I knew all women.
lift a cold latch, cold fire, cold comfort
thirty years, life's poetry gone
webs that waver and stiffen
fish nets or shrouds in corners—absence, absence.

why keep a house, how keep a world?
I heard that night
the great oak falling stroke by stroke.
I saw a face
the gentle months and years made of my face—
blinded, stoned. but pure, so pure
death weeps for it; the murderers
plucked by the hair from peace
sweat in their stocks.

Daughters
shall I be bold print of your history
blackened by votive smoke, weighed down
under your golden chains, granting
innocence to sexual joy? Mona Lisa
your smile is pure hell, impure heaven. Expedient dame
I smile as women smile when love's finesse—

a blind beggar knocks—
come in!

On hands and knees
a soot-blackened woman
pokes the new fire from ash. Distraction
of death's gimlet eye may be
that last ditch face, that stench—
nor son, nor beauty, nor familiar! the world
crawls like crabs or lepers to my door

and I began to be, in death.
And you—
no swans for guides, no gingerbread house
no metamorphosis or curse
attending
but a plain country road, smoke going up.
Hope
a man at rope's end, knocks
listens, this side or that, a door.
possible the sing-song goes
probable—and—*sesame!*

when I pass into your lives
the still life trembles—still birth
or quick? God knows. we know
only in loss.
My son
lies like an oak recumbent, not yet rotten
of whom a house is made, people and children.
I stand here
breaking a loaf for beggar men, hearing
the whine of ineffectuals, hearing
the pulled bow of the universe
the tide and fury—

broken bread, a broken house
one great loaf, rent and eaten—
resurrection!

VI

Select flora and fauna
converging
like merciful Iroquois
    in moccasins and earphones
around
you know whose
    dying camp fire

Laurel

They had 280 languages
and 4,862 local dialects
in which to say
no hope no future not a chance

when they invaded the interior
they brought along
a few phrases in pidgin
no hope no future not a chance

the savages laid aside
their feathers, beads, masks
and the gods whose painted images
adorned the moving boat

nevertheless
here and there in the dust
where man may touch the living green

I spell
like a finger
across blind deaf flesh

HOPE FUTURE CHANCE

Ski

I tried on
skins
or incarnations
the way a skier tries on
new hoods; hard green,
bull red, black.

Black once
as a rare tulip
or a great bird's
mutation
I took off—
a jump to end all! then

the usual epitaph
in black, for black;

close, but no see-gar

Walls

In no sense shoring up the wall
which stood like an old sarge
flat-footed   blank faced   clipped

bellowing his orders—
Privies to clean
murders to learn
somebody's taxes paid for   somebody's fevers

Messianic hot as Panhandle
behind every window a candle
behind every soldier a mother knitting

death heads into shawls
behind every wall
surprise!   another wall

except when you   Corita
pin a mask
where no face was   and
ready!   aim!   barks from the mastiff mouth

The wall turns to water
drops its pants in fear
runs   runs like a miler
                    to hell out of here and man

Tree

Botched together
a board fence
a neanderthal mockup

suddenly something
occurred,
ball to socket to
skull, I stood up

stood like a self willed savior
grinning, baiting big bad death

clutching my hornbook
crying to mother earth; I am!

Farm

A drain curved
like a captive swan's neck
sang, nonetheless, sweetly as the sea.
Old weeds, lilacs
made a paradigm;
in their ragged fleece
to sit and not prosper.
Two elms
stood for life and chance,
spoke no heroics.

Then, four rotted berry crates
two screen doors
a broken barrow
a compost heap,
weeds springing, bold, ripe
unkillable, voracious for life.

New heavens and a new earth
begin here, in the last hour
when evening sun
like a compassionate knowing mind
lighting on foulness, lights

the pearl in the world's sty.

Fish

a freak's eye
a cold shoulder
a dog's mouth
a green complexion—
alas for
immortal longings—

to die a hero
arms locked
fervently as a lion's
about the beloved prey—
the world   the world!

Absurd?
You have seen me
a basket case
nailed
in cold blood
to the scaling board
stinking
to high heaven

no beauty
no comeliness
a worm
alas no man.

Bread

A loaf of it shaped like **God**
drawn from a Shaker oven
brown as autumn, rich as a
barn groaning

I want to be broken in 12
pieces; shame you rabbis, you
lock me in your poorhouse
while Lazarus dies at the gate

O when will you run to him
with me singing freedom! **in your**
fruitless hands?

Butterfly

Wrapped like dead Jesus in 1) the American flag
2) Pharaoh's table cloth and 3) a prime giant
cigar leaf

I went into training for three months
arose; a deck hand, strong man, stevedore.

Wrong again! all my dreams
gone   I waver
hover, run for cover.

My big moment—
lighting on a stallion's shoulder
too feeble to be twitched off, heard
like electric shock, that black
buried engine, that well of oil or blood
struck; mine! mine!

Subway

The worm is full of people, death reversed!
I heard an old man
cry terror
his face covered with mottled hands

A gnat, an apocalypse; the subway
gathering fury as it sped—

he screamed and screamed. We pulled
like a last demented day into the Concourse;

he climbed out, ragged, resigned
the Styx traversed, immediate hell ahead.

VII

Horatio: a Short Snappy Life
or
Things Are Not Hopeless Yet, But
Be Patient, They Shortly Will Be

Baby

I pushed out of there on my tricycle
It was uphill all the way
dodging the fish they threw—
the wrong road signs, road blocks,
poltergeists, the midwife's face
red as an elbow. I tell you I just made it.

My home town Troy burned down.
When I purpose going back, it ends at a mom
who pushed under and sleeps through. *Horatio*

she whispers in my blood, *if I love you*

move it out of here, daddy

death wants you for field hand. No. You go.

Play

Said to me sternly; play the game!
and clouted me when I lost

O implacable impeccable puritan
all prefrontal
development, like an Irish
Torquemada with big driven hands
doing the right things for the
wrong reasons
                    I have forgotten
your game but in dreams
cower; seeing not you
but your big hands so right
so wrong at the
reins or sputtering fuses of the world

Heart

When I was a city kid, we had a game
from roof to roof, follow the leader.
It brought the heart running
out of its cotton picking cage to see the view—
a span of pigeons going up
like a hand describing flight,
the docks, Murphy's overalls jigging on the clothesline.

We jumped as though
a second ago
were hot asphalt,
too hot to stand on. And my heart climbed out and
watched and flew!

For God's sake
don't cage the pigeons. They stink there and moult
turn grey as ash cans, end up dead.

Sun

always comes on strong
Horatio, the preacher said,
even, preferable, after a bad start.
God says so, he thumped, *so do I!*
(In whose interest
the sun damn sight better had!)

But Rev. Potash addressed an audience
in the Poconos; whereas our
Alger, creeping about under Con Edison's
tarry mantle,
and Big Burning Brother
slogging it above,
never quite
actually
            made
                  connection.

God

Lined up like easter eggs
inside grandfather
there we were!

every hour on the hour
he'd take out his conductor's
stick, crack our
bald heads, cry
OK kids, onstage!

we were integrated
all right; 24 was
Congolese; 12 named
Endeavor, white as
high noon.
They came out
like two altar boys
on a funeral director's
calendar.

There was 10 o'clock
Scholar, and 4 A.M.,
a glassy-eyed junkie
and someone else
under a sheet
d.o.a.
his watch stopped
like an unwound heart

Another cried another laughed
a blind kid improvised
on a flute

then me; Horatio, I
oiled the works and
brought the old man his beer

Holiday

One July
I hung balls on Christmas trees
and folded the Daily News
cunningly—

generals' cornets
newsprint airplanes
soggy submarines.
gifts
for the torrid newborn god—

The bible text of that day
commended
by a ghostly father;

be ye eunuchs
for the kingdom of god.

City

Imagine a Toltec city
built for fun; pyramids,
flowers, star gazing. And a
game; the first, they say
ancestor of the National League;
a raw rubber ball and ring.

Anyway
you take it
history is not always all
roses; i.e.,
the losing team
never reached home and mother, was

eaten for dinner.

I ask the score
stooping at the dugout;
Toltecs, what price fun? Who won?

Smile

Not round enough
to eat whole
the old red
fruit or its worm

I
WIDEN
when eyes swim toward
like fish, head on

singing like fish;

*I'd like to teach
you to swim too*

jump in, come true.

My Guts Begin

        like white trash
come into money

grumbling at
slum lords; *huh!*
you ain't much

we'll march right out
someday; worms
turn, you better

believe it. This hole!
bad plumbing, place
stinks, less and less

daylight, rats free-
loading. Just wait that
lease runs

out
soon O
soon

Sex

When I was 48
daddy squeaked from his
wheel chair, *Horatio*
its time you and the facts
got together. Bring me
that box from the deal
shelf. Sit down.

(had managed
quite well to then—
white mice
eskimo pies
Stanley Steamer
yodeling club.)

He took out two
stuffed birds, m. & f., two
murderous
model bees
with buzzers in their ———.
Last, I blush to tell,
an unclothed wooden doll,
not a boy. Rasped: *now*
get this.

That transpired yesterday
He expired today.
I am consuming as usual, my
curds and whey.

Death

He was on stilts
fifty miles high
with a big paper
sunflower for eye

said with a grin
taking me in his arms
well
Horatio
how do things look
from up here?